WITHDRAWN

Holidays and Celebrations

St. Patrick's Day

by Brenda Haugen
illustrated by Sheree Boyd

Thanks to our advisers for their expertise, research, and advice:

Alexa Sandmann, Ed.D., Professor of Literacy
The University of Toledo, Toledo, Ohio
Member, National Council for the Social Studies

Susan Kesselring, M.A., Literacy Educator
Rosemount-Apple Valley-Eagan (Minnesota) School District

PICTURE WINDOW BOOKS
MINNEAPOLIS, MINNESOTA

For Kevin and the Sandahls. I'm lucky to have you in my life!

Managing Editor: Bob Temple
Creative Director: Terri Foley
Editor: Sara E. Hoffmann
Editorial Adviser: Andrea Cascardi
Copy Editor: Laurie Kahn
Designer: Melissa Voda
Page production: The Design Lab
The illustrations in this book were rendered digitally.

Picture Window Books
5115 Excelsior Boulevard
Suite 232
Minneapolis, MN 55416
1-877-845-8392
www.picturewindowbooks.com

Printed in the United States of America.

Library of Congress Cataloging-in-Publication Data
Haugen, Brenda.
St. patrick's day / by Brenda Haugen ; illustrated by Sheree Boyd.
p. cm. — (Holidays and celebrations)
Summary: Briefly discusses the history and customs connected to the celebration
of St. Patrick's Day. Includes bibliographical references.
ISBN 1-4048-0197-9
1. St. patrick's day—Juvenile literature. [1. St. patrick's day. 2. Holidays.] I. Boyd,
Sheree, ill. II. Title. III. Holidays and celebrations (Picture Window Books)
GT4995.P3 .H38 2004
394.262—dc21
2003006104

Strike up the band and join the parade.
Grab something green to wear.

3

Do you feel lucky?
It's March 17—St. Patrick's Day!

Happy
St. Patrick's
Day

St. Patrick's Day celebrates
the traditions of Ireland.
It also celebrates a man
named St. Patrick.

St. Patrick did many great things for the Irish people.

Long ago, most people in Ireland could not read or write. St. Patrick wanted to help them learn. He wanted them to become Christians, too.

An old story says that St. Patrick used shamrocks to teach people about Christianity. He explained that, just as the shamrock has three leaves, Christians believe God is three things in one.

A shamrock is a clover with three leaves. It is a symbol of luck in Ireland. The shamrock also has become a symbol of St. Patrick's Day.

When St. Patrick died,
the people of Ireland were very sad.
The church made him a saint.

St. Patrick's Day celebrates his life.
It is a holy day in Ireland.

Many people in Ireland go to church on St. Patrick's Day.

Canada

The United States

In the 1800s, many Irish people moved
to the United States and Canada.
They came because there was
not enough food in their country.

The Irish brought their stories and customs with them to their new homes. They brought St. Patrick's Day, too.

Ireland

England

France

One Irish story tells about elves called leprechauns. Leprechauns have hidden pots of gold. People say leprechauns hide their gold at the end of the rainbow.

The leprechaun is one
of the symbols of Ireland.

St. Patrick's Day is celebrated by many Americans. Some people wear green on this holiday.

Many Irish people display the flag of Ireland on St. Patrick's Day. They do this to celebrate the country of their ancestors.

Some people even dye their food and drinks green!

Many parades spread good cheer on St. Patrick's Day. Some of the biggest are in New York, Boston, and Chicago.

More than 100 U.S. cities have St. Patrick's Day parades!

An old saying says that everyone is Irish on St. Patrick's Day.

Patrick Day

So grab something green. Join in the fun.

Watch for leprechauns.
It may be your lucky day!

It is a custom to wish people "the luck of the Irish." If you say this to your friends and family, you are wishing them good luck.

21

You Can Make a Shamrock Shaker

What you need:

scissors

one or two sheets of
  green construction paper

2 paper plates

glue

stapler

dried beans

What you do:

1. Make sure you have an adult to help you.

2. Cut three circles out of the green construction paper. The circles should be about four inches (10 centimeters) wide.

3. Cut a stem out of the green construction paper.

4. Arrange the circles and stem into the shape of a shamrock on the back side of one of the paper plates. Glue them in place.

5. Staple the second plate to the plate with the shamrock picture on it. The back sides of both plates should face the outside. Be sure to leave a small opening at the top of the plates.

6. Drop a few dried beans through the opening.

7. Staple the opening so that the beans are sealed between the plates.

8. Your shamrock shaker is ready to shake!

Fun Facts

- Did you know there are no snakes in Ireland? An old story says that St. Patrick sent all the snakes away.

- Ireland is one of the largest islands in the world.

- Ireland is nicknamed the Emerald Isle. This is because emeralds are green and Ireland's land is very green. Ireland's land is green because it often rains there.

- When St. Patrick was young, he was a slave. He was taken from his home and made to work. After six hard years, he escaped. He decided to spend the rest of his life helping others.

- The Blarney stone is a famous rock in an Irish tower. Many people kiss the Blarney stone. Old stories say this will make them good talkers.

Words to Know

ancestor—a member of your family who lived a long time ago

Christian—a person who follows the teachings of Jesus Christ

emerald—a beautiful gem that is green in color

saint—a person honored by the Catholic church for his or her holiness

shamrock—a green clover with three leaves

slave—a person who is owned by another person

To Learn More

At the Library

Burnett, Bernice. **The First Book of Holidays**. New York: F. Watts, 1974.

Gibbons, Gail. **St. Patrick's Day**. New York: Holiday House, 1994.

Roop, Peter and Connie. **Let's Celebrate St. Patrick's Day**. Brookfield, Conn.: Millbrook Press, 2003.

Schuh, Mari C. **St. Patrick's Day**. Mankato, Minn.: Pebble Books, 2003.

Van Straalen, Alice. **The Book of Holidays Around the World**. New York: Dutton, 1986.

Fact Hound

Fact Hound offers a safe, fun way to find Web sites related to this book. All of the sites on Fact Hound have been researched by our staff.
http://www.facthound.com

1. Visit the Fact Hound home page.
2. Enter a search word related to this book, or type in this special code: 1404801979.
3. Click on the FETCH IT button.

Your trusty Fact Hound will fetch the best sites for you!

Index

24